THE COMPLETE GUIDE TO MICROWAVE COOKING 2023

Discover Everything You Need to Know About Cooking Quick, Convenient Nutrient-Rich Food with Over 75 Delectable Recipes

Sarah Jordan, LD, CCN

COPYRIGHT PAGE

Copyright © 2023 by Sarah Jordan, LD, CCN

All rights reserved. Except for brief quotations contained in reviews or other noncommercial uses permitted by copyright law, no part of this publication may be reproduced, distributed, or transmitted in any form or by any means, including photocopying, recording, or other electronic or mechanical methods, without the prior written permission of the publisher.

The information and recipes in The Complete Guide to Microwave Cooking 2023 are not meant to replace professional medical or nutritional advice and are provided solely for educational reasons. The author and publisher disclaim all liability for any harm that may come from following the advice in this book. Before making any modifications to one's diet or beginning a program to lose weight, it is recommended that the reader seek the advice of a healthcare provider or nutritionist.

Table of Contents

COPYRIGHT PAGE 2

Table of Contents 3

CHAPTER I: INTRODUCTION 1

    What is Microwave Cooking? 3

    Benefits of Microwave Cooking 5

CHAPTER II: PREPARING YOUR KITCHEN FOR MICROWAVE COOKING 9

    Tools and Equipment 12

    Stocking Microwave Friendly Ingredients 15

CHAPTER III: STRATEGIES FOR EFFORTLESS MICROWAVE MEALS 19

    Customizing Microwave Cooking to Your Dietary Needs 22

CHAPTER IV: NUTRIENT-RICH RECIPES YOU CAN TRY 26

NUTRIENT-RICH BREAKFAST RECIPES 27

Oatmeal with Fruits and Nuts: 27

Breakfast Burrito: 28

Instant Cinnamon Rolls: 29

Microwave Scrambled Eggs with Spinach and Feta: ... 30

Microwave Breakfast Sandwich: 31

Microwaved Quiche with Veggies and Cheese: 32

Greek Yogurt Parfait: 33

Microwaveable Breakfast Hash: 33

Rice Pudding with Cinnamon and Raisins: 35

Microwaved Breakfast Quesadilla: 36

French Toast in a Mug: 37

Microwaveable Breakfast Wrap: 38

Breakfast Mug Cake: 39

Microwaved Sweet Potato with Almond Butter and Banana: 40

Veggie-Packed Microwave Frittata: 41

NUTRIENT-RICH LUNCH RECIPES 43

Microwaveable Macaroni and Cheese: 43

Stuffed Baked Potato with Toppings: 44

Microwaved Vegetable Stir-Fry with Tofu: 45

Instant Cup Noodles or Ramen: 46

Microwaved Leftovers from Dinner: 47

Microwaveable Chicken or Veggie Wrap: 48

Quick Microwave Burrito Bowl: 49

Microwaved Spinach and Feta Stuffed Chicken Breast: 50

Instant Microwaveable Soup or Chili: 51

Microwaveable Vegetable Lasagna: 52

Microwaved Quinoa and Black Bean Bowl: 53

Teriyaki Chicken with Steamed Rice: 54

Microwaved Stuffed Bell Peppers: 55

Microwaveable Pasta with Marinara Sauce and Vegetables: 56

Quick Microwave Quesadilla with Cheese and Beans: 57

Microwaved Egg Fried Rice with Veggies: 58

NUTRIENT-RICH DINNER RECIPES 60

Microwaved Baked Potato with Toppings: 60

Instant Microwaveable Dinner Entrée: 61

Microwaved Chicken and Vegetable Stir-Fry: 61

Quick Microwave Pasta with Sauce: 62

Microwaved Stuffed Bell Peppers: 63

Microwaveable Beef or Vegetable Stew: 65

Microwaved Salmon with Lemon and Herbs: 65

Instant Microwaveable Pizza: 66

Microwaveable Vegetable Curry with Rice: 67

Microwaved Sweet and Sour Chicken: 68

Microwaved Spinach and Cheese Stuffed Pasta: 69

Quick Microwave Ramen Bowl with Veggies and Protein: 70

Microwaveable Chicken or Vegetable Pot Pie: 71

Microwaved Quinoa and Roasted Vegetables: 71

Microwaveable Black Bean and Corn Enchiladas: 72

NUTRIENT-RICH SNACK RECIPES 74

Microwaveable Popcorn: 74

Warm Nachos with Melted Cheese: 75

Microwaved Baked Apple with Cinnamon: 76

Mini Microwave Mug Cake: 77

Toasted Microwave Quesadilla with Cheese: 78

Microwaved Mixed Nuts with Spices: 79

Quick Microwave Potato Chips: 80

Microwaved Mozzarella Sticks: 81

Warm Nut Butter on Rice Cakes: 82

Microwaveable Trail Mix with Dried Fruits: 83

Microwaved Mini Pizza on English Muffin: 84

Melted Chocolate-Dipped Strawberries: 85

Microwaved Yogurt and Granola Parfait: 86

Toasted Microwave Pita Chips with Hummus: 87

Quick Microwave Oat Bars: 88

NUTRIENT-RICH DESSERT REICPES 90

Warm Chocolate Chip Cookie in a Mug: 90

Microwaved Apple Crisp with Oats: 91

Quick Microwave Brownie in a Mug: 93

Instant Microwaveable Chocolate Pudding: 94

Microwaved Banana Split with Toppings: 95

Warm Fruit Cobbler with Ice Cream: 96

Microwaved Rice Pudding with Cinnamon: 97

Microwaveable S'mores Dip: 98

Easy Microwave Caramel Popcorn: 99

Microwaved Bread Pudding with Raisins: 100

Quick Microwave Berry Crumble: 101

Microwaved Chocolate-Covered Strawberries: 102

Warm Cinnamon Roll in a Mug: 103

Microwaveable Cheesecake in a Cup: 104

Microwaved Fruit Fondue with Chocolate: 105

CHAPTER V: FINAL NOTES BEFORE YOU GO! 107

Exploring Nutrient-Rich Ingredients 109

CHAPTER I: INTRODUCTION

You are about to go on a culinary journey that will change your perspective on the art of cooking forever. In these pages, we cast off the shackles of the traditional kitchen and enter the wondrous realm of microwave cooking. Get ready to be blown away as we reveal the secrets of this simple kitchen tool, opening the door to a world of quick, easy, and shockingly exquisite foods that will change the way you cook forever.

Reheating leftovers and making popcorn in a microwave is only the beginning. It's a dynamic cooking method that allows you to make gourmet-level meals in a fraction of the time. Along the way, we'll learn how to make healthy, delicious, and visually beautiful meals using just a microwave oven, expanding our horizons well beyond the realm of packaged convenience foods.

This cookbook opens up a world of possibilities, whether you're a busy professional looking for an alternative to takeout, a college student with restricted kitchen access, or someone who just enjoys the art of efficient cooking. With the speed and accuracy of microwave cooking, we'll investigate a wide variety of dishes, from filling breakfasts and satisfying main meals to pleasant snacks and tempting desserts.

But there's more to this cookbook than just recipes. It's a manual for getting the most out of your microwave, from learning how to use it safely to picking out the best equipment. Discover the science behind the magic, and develop the courage to experiment and create your own microwave masterpieces, all while learning how to modify standard recipes for the microwave.

Don't have negative associations with microwave meals. To innovation, efficiency, and deliciousness, we set sail today. Get ready to have your mind blown and your microwave cooking skills skyrocketed to a new level of mastery. This cookbook will show you how to make the most of your microwave, making it an indispensable tool in the kitchen. Enter the future of food preparation with me as I introduce you to the wonders of the microwave oven.

What is Microwave Cooking?

The use of electromagnetic waves to rapidly heat and cook food is the basis of the microwave cooking method. The heart of this technique is the generation of electromagnetic radiation, often known as microwaves, using a microwave oven, a ubiquitous household equipment. The water molecules in the meal are quickly vibrated by the penetrating microwaves. The food is cooked or reheated because the vibrations create heat.

Microwave cooking is popular because it is so fast and easy to use. Microwaves may quickly heat food, in contrast to conventional stovetop or oven cooking methods that typically call for preheating and lengthy cooking periods. This makes it a great option for people who are in need of a fast lunch throughout their hectic schedule.

Cooking with a microwave not only saves time, but also energy. Using a full oven or stovetop burner might be wasteful of energy when preparing food the traditional way.

In contrast, microwave cooking's efficient use of energy comes from its focused heating.

Although most people use microwaves to reheat previously cooked meals, they have many other applications in the kitchen. Vegetables and potatoes may be boiled or roasted, delicate fish fillets can be poached, and even desserts can be whipped up with this method. More and more innovative microwave-friendly recipes that accommodate a wide range of dietary restrictions and preferences are being created all the time.

To get the most of your microwave, you should familiarize yourself with its quirks and quirks. Depending on the microwave's wattage and other factors, some foods may cook more evenly than others. It's important to try multiple cooking periods, power settings, and containers that can hold various foods for the best results.

As we learn more about microwave cooking, we're able to debunk the myth that it can only be used to make mediocre or quick meals. When used properly, the microwave can be a fantastic cooking tool, allowing you to whip up delicious, healthy meals in a flash. It's the perfect combination of cutting-edge science and delicious cuisine, unlocking a door to speedy meals that fit in with busy schedules. If you're searching for a fast evening meal or just want to try something new in the kitchen, microwave cooking has a lot to offer.

Benefits of Microwave Cooking

The advent of microwave ovens has been a welcome addition to many homes and busy schedules. Microwave cooking has risen to prominence in homes throughout the world not just because it is quick and easy to use, but also because of the many benefits it provides.

The extraordinary quickness of microwave cooking is one of its most obvious advantages. In today's fast-paced society, being able to prepare a dinner in a short amount of time might make all the difference. In contrast to more conventional cooking methods, microwave ovens create heat directly into the meal. This effectiveness is especially helpful for people who are often on the go, as it reduces the time required to prepare meals from hours to minutes.

Microwave cooking's energy savings is a major selling point. Preheating a whole oven or stovetop burner for a smaller meal is sometimes unnecessary when using conventional cooking methods. On the other hand, microwaves heat the food from the inside out, resulting in less energy use, lower utility costs, and a less environmental impact.

Microwave ovens are a great option for those who are concerned about keeping their meals' nutritional value intact because of their use of rapid cooking times. Microwave cooking, due to its quick and targeted heating, can preserve more of a dish's vitamins and minerals than other cooking methods, which might include longer contact to heat and water.

The cleaning time after microwaving a meal is also short. Spills and splatters can be avoided by using microwave-safe containers and covering plates with microwave-safe lids or wraps. This reduces the number of dishes that need to be washed after cooking.

College students and those who live in small apartments might especially benefit from the microwave's portability and ease of use when it comes to preparing meals. Many healthy and fulfilling meals may be prepared in a microwave oven without the need of a stove or other conventional cooking methods.

In addition, microwaves are a great resource for culinary exploration and innovation. Adapting classic dishes to the microwave is a fun way to experiment with new flavors and techniques. Because of its adaptability, people can make everything from simple breakfasts to elaborate meals and sweet treats.

In conclusion, microwave cooking has several advantages beyond its portability. This cooking method is advantageous since it requires less time, energy, and water to prepare meals while keeping most of the nutrients intact. Its versatility and adaptability make it an indispensable tool for people with hectic schedules who want to eat healthily and try new recipes. Microwave cooking has changed the way we think about and approach making meals as we try to keep up with the pace and variety of modern living.

CHAPTER II: PREPARING YOUR KITCHEN FOR MICROWAVE COOKING

To get the most of your microwave cooking and simplify your culinary experience, you need take the time to set up your kitchen properly. A well-stocked kitchen allows you to make a wide range of tasty foods using your microwave, maximizing its potential for speed and convenience.

Check out what you already have in the way of kitchen tools. Safe and efficient microwave cooking requires the use of microwave-safe containers. Try to find microwave-friendly or microwave-specific containers. The containers won't bend or give out dangerous chemicals even when subjected to the high temperatures created by cooking. You may want to have a variety of sizes and shapes so that you may use them with a wide range of foods.

Microwave-safe wraps and containers are just as vital. These will keep your microwave neat and tidy and reduce the amount of time spent cleaning it up. Ventilated plastic wraps or microwave-safe lids are great options for heating food in the microwave. The food will stay wet and cook evenly thanks to the vents in the covers.

Purchase cooking implements that can be used in a microwave. If you want to keep your microwave in good working order, you should avoid using any metal utensils or cookware in it. Instead, use microwave-safe cutlery made of materials like glass, ceramic, or microwave-safe plastics. The microwave is safe for use with wooden utensils, and they won't do any damage to the oven's inside.

You should get a thermometer that can be used in a microwave. With this device, you can check the doneness and safety of your food by tracking its inside temperature while it cooks. In order to avoid undercooked or overcooked meat and poultry, it is crucial to have a thermometer on available while cooking.

Make space in your kitchen for a microwave and use it as such. The easiest way to prepare a dinner using a microwave is to have everything you need right next to it. With this set up in place, you won't have to stop what you're doing to go find the right pot or pan while you're in the middle of preparing a meal.

Finally, learn how to properly operate your microwave's controls. You can get the best results by learning how to modify the cooking time and power level for your specific microwave. Learn the intricacies of your microwave by trying out various settings and cooking times.

In conclusion, getting your kitchen set up for microwave cooking entails acquiring the necessary equipment and supplies. Each component, from microwave-safe containers and covers to utensils and a thermometer, is essential to the success and enjoyment of microwave cooking. With a well-stocked kitchen, you may quickly and easily experiment with the wide variety of recipes possible with this cutting-edge culinary technique.

Tools and Equipment

When it comes to cooking in a microwave, having the proper implements at your disposal is essential for producing tasty and satisfying results. These gadgets not only make cooking easier and safer, but they also give you a lot of room to experiment and be creative.

Containers that can survive the high temperatures generated by microwave ovens without warping or releasing dangerous chemicals into your food are the backbone of microwave cooking. Try to find microwave-safe plastic, glass, or ceramic containers. Having a selection of sizes and shapes at your disposal makes it possible to prepare everything from leftovers to whole dinners with ease.

Wraps and coverings designed for use in the microwave prevent food from drying out and ensure consistent cooking by trapping in moisture. Covers with vents or those can be heated in the microwave are great choices. Dishes can also be covered with microwave-safe plastic wraps meant for use in the microwave, which will allow steam to escape while keeping the mess contained.

Choose utensils that won't cause sparks or melt the microwave, such as silicone or plastic. The best materials to use are glass, ceramic, and microwave-safe plastics. You may use wooden spoons and forks in the microwave without worrying about damaging the appliance.

A microwave-safe thermometer is an invaluable kitchen tool for checking the doneness of meat and poultry when microwaving. This guarantees that the meal is cooked to the right doneness and is safe to eat.

A turntable, or revolving glass plate, used in many microwave ovens, helps to properly disperse microwave energy throughout the food being cooked. The need for constant stirring or rotating is eliminated, leading to more uniform cooking.

Having microwave-safe bowls and mugs on hand allows you to do more with your microwave, from reheating soups to baking mug cakes.

Baking plates made specifically for use in the microwave are a must-have for anybody who enjoys microwave baking.

These dishes are designed to endure high heat and typically have handles.

Vegetables and other items may be steamed in the microwave safely when placed in a microwave-safe plastic bag. Use only microwave-safe bags to keep potentially dangerous substances out of your food.

Covers for plates that may be heated in the microwave are used to avoid messy spills when reheating meals. They are versatile, as they may be used for a wide variety of dish sizes.

While the use of microwave-friendly containers lessens the likelihood of burns, it is still prudent to keep a set of microwave oven gloves or pads on hand for safe handling of anything heated in the microwave.

The best way to maximize the usefulness of your microwave oven is to consult a cookbook or other recipe resource specifically designed for microwave cooking.

With the correct accessories, a microwave may be used for everything from quick reheating to elaborate culinary creations. If you buy good microwaveable things and learn how to utilize them, the world of microwave cooking opens up to you with countless delicious options.

Stocking Microwave Friendly Ingredients

Preparing for efficient and novel microwave cooking by stocking up on microwave-friendly items is a smart move. While it's true that microwaves save time, having all the necessary components on hand guarantees that you'll be able to prepare healthy and satisfying meals in a flash.

veggies Broccoli, carrots, bell peppers, spinach, and zucchini are just few of the fresh veggies you should always have on hand. You may make a healthy side dish or a foundation for a more complex dinner by simply steaming or microwaving these veggies.

Vegetables that have been frozen maintain their nutritional content while providing a quick and easy meal choice. They are perfect for adding vibrancy and health benefits to your recipes because they can be cooked straight from the freezer in the microwave.

Lean Proteins: Boneless chicken breasts, fish fillets, and tofu are all microwave-safe protein options. These are ready in minutes and add protein to side dishes, wraps, and salads.

Keep a variety of precooked grains on hand, such as quinoa, brown rice, or whole wheat couscous, to make meal preparation a breeze. You may make a whole dinner by combining these grains with microwave-friendly veggies and protein sources.

Black beans, chickpeas, and kidney beans are just some of the canned beans that may be easily rewarmed in the microwave and tossed into salads, wraps, or soups for an extra dose of protein and fiber.

Whether you want your eggs scrambled, poached, or in an omelette, heating them in the microwave is a fast and easy option. Eggs can be used in savory and sweet preparations alike.

Pasta that can be cooked in a microwave, such as microwaveable pasta bowls, is a great foundation for pasta salads and other quick meals.

Sauces and condiments like marinara, teriyaki, and vinaigrettes that can be heated in the microwave should be stocked. These may be used to add depth of flavor to recipes with minimal effort.

Apples and pears, for example, may be cooked in the microwave with a sprinkling of cinnamon for a warm dessert or snack since they are microwave safe. Smoothies and porridge can benefit from the addition of frozen berries.

Almonds, walnuts, and chia seeds, among others, can be used to give microwaved foods a satisfying crunch and nutty flavor. You may improve the taste and healthfulness of your dishes by using these components.

Microwave popcorn is a convenient and tasty snack that can be prepared in a matter of minutes. It's a much better option than buying boxed snacks from the shop.

Flavoring your microwave meals is easy with a well-stocked spice cupboard. Have on hand a number of different spices and herbs, such as garlic powder, oregano, thyme, and basil.

Leftovers may be easily reheated in the microwave if they are stored in microwave-safe containers. In addition to helping the environment, this also makes it easy to prepare healthy meals.

Stocking your microwave with these items allows you to whip up a variety of nutritious and delicious meals without sacrificing quality. Because of the microwave's versatility and ease of use, equipping your kitchen is essential to making the most of this appliance.

CHAPTER III: STRATEGIES FOR EFFORTLESS MICROWAVE MEALS

Acing the skill of seamless microwave cooking calls for a methodical strategy that integrates gastronomic expertise with the freedom to explore. Making dinner may be a breeze with a few adjustments in approach that are catered to the specifics of microwave cooking.

Preparation is the essential to good microwave cooking, just as it is with traditional cooking. To save time in the kitchen, prep foods like veggies, meat, and cereals ahead of time. Meal preparation is simplified when all of the necessary components are on hand.

Make use of microwaveable bowls, plates, and utensils of the highest quality. The containers you use in the microwave should be specifically labeled as such and should be constructed of materials that will not deform or emit dangerous chemicals when heated.

Most microwaves have a selectable number of power settings; familiarize yourself with them. It's crucial that you know your ingredients and adjust the heat accordingly. Defrosting, mild reheating, and cooking delicate products call for lower power levels, while speedy meals benefit from higher settings.

To ensure that food is cooked evenly in the microwave, it is a good idea to stir or turn the dish every few minutes. When reheating bigger products or those of irregular shapes, this is especially crucial.

When using a microwave, it's best to layer your ingredients such that the components that take the longest to cook are closest to the center of the dish. You might want to plan your cooking sessions around different meal times.

Splatters can be avoided and moisture can be retained by covering food with a microwave-safe cover or wrap before placing it in the microwave. Some foods may also require venting so that steam may escape during cooking. Try different combinations of lids and vents to see what works best with your dish.

When trying out new recipes, it's important to keep a close watch on the cooking time. Undercooking can cause uneven cooking while overcooking can make food tough or rubbery.

If you need to microwave a large amount of food at once, try doing it in batches. This way, you can keep an eye on the cooking progress and make sure everything is done at the same time.

Reheating, defrosting, steaming, and rapid cooking are some of the many jobs at which microwaves truly shine. To save time and effort, use the microwave for these specialized tasks.

Don't be afraid to branch out from tried-and-true methods and try something new. Try out new ingredients, flavor profiles, and preparation methods. Use your imagination and make anything from a fast cup cake to a new method to cook veggies.

Microwave meals taste best when they are prepared in their simplest form. Choose simple recipes that highlight fewer ingredients and fewer processes to bring out the most in each ingredient's taste.

The key to effortless microwave cooking is striking a balance between research and trial and error. You can unlock the full potential of microwave cooking by incorporating these ideas into your routine, turning ordinary ingredients into delectable and fulfilling meals with unprecedented simplicity.

Customizing Microwave Cooking to Your Dietary Needs

Adapting microwave cooking to your unique dietary demands allows you to take advantage of this cooking method while still meeting your nutritional requirements. Because of its versatility, microwave cooking may be adapted to meet the demands of those with special diets or dietary restrictions.

Microwave cooking provides a wide variety of low-carb and keto-friendly alternatives for people on these diets. Pair fast-cooked lean meats like chicken, fish, or cattle with non-starchy greens like kale, broccoli, and cauliflower. Test out some keto-friendly sweets and treats like almond flour mug cakes and chia seed puddings.

Vegan and plant-based diets will find the convenience and speed of microwave cooking very appealing. Prepare quinoa or other grains, steam or simmer a wide range of veggies, and play around with different legumes like lentils and chickpeas. Make delicious sauces and spreads by combining nut butters, tahini, and vegetable oils.

Microwaving food that does not contain gluten is a safe and time-saving option. Rice, gluten-free pasta, and potatoes can all be cooked in a microwave. Eat more gluten-free grains like quinoa, rice, and oats, and stick to full, unadulterated products.

Microwave cooking is ideal for preparing paleo-friendly meals since it allows you to use fresh, unprocessed ingredients. Simple spices go a long way when cooking meats, fish, and poultry. Ideally served with steamed or roasted veggies and some healthy fats like avocado or almonds.

Microwave cooking makes it simple to whip up dairy-free substitutes. Plant-based milk may be used to make dairy-free yogurt, while coconut milk and cashew cream can be used to make dairy-free sauces.

Microwave cooking is your friend if you're trying to eat healthfully but are short on time. Prepare lean meats, veggies, and grains ahead of time by precooking them. Make well-rounded dishes by blending these ingredients with various seasonings, sauces, and marinades.

Microwave cooking is great for portion management since it lets you make single servings or lesser amounts quickly and easily. Those who are trying to watch their calorie intake or engage in mindful eating will benefit greatly from this.

Cooking in a microwave oven, where allergens may be avoided by carefully monitoring the cooking process, is one method for effectively managing food allergies and sensitivities. Use a different set of utensils and storage containers for food that is free of allergens.

Many time-honored dishes can be prepared in a microwave. Examples include microwave "baked" potatoes and microwave frittatas. Try with different combinations of components to see what works best for your diet.

By adapting microwave cooking to your specific nutritional needs, you may save time in the kitchen while also making nutritious meals. Thanks to the microwave's versatility, you may eat a varied and enjoyable meal even if you have special dietary needs. As you venture into the world of microwave-friendly recipes, you'll find an abundance of options that are harmonious with your diet plan.

CHAPTER IV: NUTRIENT-RICH RECIPES YOU CAN TRY

NUTRIENT-RICH BREAKFAST RECIPES

Oatmeal with Fruits and Nuts:

Ingredients

1/2 cup rolled oats

1 cup milk (dairy or non-dairy)

1/2 banana, sliced

Handful of berries (e.g., blueberries, strawberries)

Handful of chopped nuts (e.g., almonds, walnuts)

Instructions

In a microwave-safe bowl, combine the oats and milk.

Microwave on high for 2-3 minutes, stirring halfway through.

Top with sliced banana, berries, and chopped nuts. Enjoy!

Breakfast Burrito:

Ingredients

2 large eggs

1/4 cup diced bell peppers

1/4 cup diced onions

1/4 cup shredded cheese

2 small flour tortillas

Instructions

In a microwave-safe bowl, whisk the eggs, bell peppers, and onions.

Microwave on medium-high for 1-2 minutes, stirring halfway through, until the eggs are cooked.

Place the scrambled eggs onto the tortillas, sprinkle with cheese, and roll them up into burritos.

Instant Cinnamon Rolls:

Ingredients

1 can refrigerated cinnamon rolls

Instructions

Place the cinnamon rolls on a microwave-safe plate.

Microwave according to the package instructions. Typically, it's around 1 minute per roll.

Drizzle the included icing over the warm rolls and enjoy.

Microwave Scrambled Eggs with Spinach and Feta:

Ingredients

2 large eggs

Handful of fresh spinach

2 tbsp crumbled feta cheese

Instructions

In a microwave-safe bowl, whisk the eggs.

Stir in the fresh spinach and microwave on medium-high for 1-2 minutes, stirring occasionally.

Sprinkle feta cheese on top and serve.

Microwave Breakfast Sandwich:

Ingredients

1 English muffin, split and toasted

1 large egg

1 slice cheese

1 slice cooked ham or bacon

Instructions

Crack the egg into a microwave-safe bowl and beat it.

Microwave on high for 30 seconds, then stir. Continue microwaving in 15-second intervals until the egg is cooked.

Place the cooked egg, cheese, and ham/bacon between the toasted English muffin halves.

Microwaved Quiche with Veggies and Cheese:

Ingredients

2 large eggs

2 tbsp milk

2 tbsp diced vegetables (e.g., bell peppers, onions)

2 tbsp shredded cheese

Salt and pepper to taste

Instructions

In a microwave-safe mug, whisk the eggs and milk.

Stir in diced vegetables, cheese, salt, and pepper.

Microwave on medium-high for 1-2 minutes, or until the quiche is set.

Greek Yogurt Parfait:

Ingredients

1/2 cup Greek yogurt

1/4 cup granola

Handful of mixed berries

Instructions

Layer Greek yogurt, granola, and mixed berries in a microwave-safe bowl.

Microwave on medium for 30 seconds to slightly warm the yogurt and berries. Enjoy!

Microwaveable Breakfast Hash:

Ingredients

1 small potato, diced

1/4 cup diced bell peppers

1/4 cup diced onions

1/4 cup cooked sausage or bacon, chopped

Salt and pepper to taste

Instructions

In a microwave-safe bowl, combine the diced potato, bell peppers, and onions.

Microwave on high for 3-4 minutes, stirring occasionally, until the potato is tender.

Stir in the cooked sausage or bacon, and season with salt and pepper.

Rice Pudding with Cinnamon and Raisins:

Ingredients

1/2 cup cooked rice

1 cup milk (dairy or non-dairy)

2 tbsp sugar

1/4 tsp ground cinnamon

2 tbsp raisins

Instructions

In a microwave-safe bowl, combine the cooked rice, milk, sugar, and cinnamon.

Microwave on medium-high for 3-4 minutes, stirring occasionally, until the mixture thickens.

Stir in raisins and let it cool slightly before enjoying.

Microwaved Breakfast Quesadilla:

Ingredients

2 small flour tortillas

1/4 cup shredded cheese

2 large eggs

2 tbsp salsa

Instructions

Place one tortilla on a microwave-safe plate and sprinkle half of the shredded cheese on it.

Crack the eggs onto the tortilla and whisk them slightly to spread.

Top with the remaining cheese and the second tortilla.

Microwave on medium-high for 2-3 minutes, until the eggs are cooked and the cheese is melted.

Cut into wedges and serve with salsa.

French Toast in a Mug:

Ingredients

1 slice bread, cubed

1 large egg

1/4 cup milk (dairy or non-dairy)

1/2 tsp vanilla extract

Pinch of ground cinnamon

Instructions

In a microwave-safe mug, whisk the egg, milk, vanilla extract, and ground cinnamon.

Add the cubed bread and press it down to soak in the mixture.

Microwave on medium-high for 1-2 minutes, until the mixture is set.

Microwaveable Breakfast Wrap:

Ingredients

1 large tortilla

2 large eggs

1/4 cup black beans (cooked and drained)

2 tbsp salsa

Instructions

In a microwave-safe bowl, whisk the eggs and microwave on medium-high for 1-2 minutes, stirring occasionally, until cooked.

Warm the tortilla in the microwave for 10-15 seconds.

Spread the cooked eggs and black beans onto the tortilla, and top with salsa.

Roll up the tortilla to make a wrap.

Breakfast Mug Cake:

Ingredients

1/4 cup quick oats

1 ripe banana, mashed

1 large egg

1/4 tsp baking powder

Pinch of cinnamon

Instructions

In a microwave-safe mug, mix the mashed banana and egg until well combined.

Stir in the oats, baking powder, and cinnamon.

Microwave on high for 1-2 minutes, until the cake is set.

Microwaved Sweet Potato with Almond Butter and Banana:

Ingredients

1 small sweet potato

1 tbsp almond butter

1/2 banana, sliced

Instructions

Pierce the sweet potato with a fork a few times and microwave on high for 4-6 minutes, until tender.

Split the sweet potato open and top with almond butter and banana slices.

Veggie-Packed Microwave Frittata:

Ingredients

2 large eggs

2 tbsp milk (dairy or non-dairy)

1/4 cup diced vegetables (e.g., bell peppers, spinach, tomatoes)

2 tbsp shredded cheese

Salt and pepper to taste

Instructions

In a microwave-safe bowl, whisk the eggs and milk.

Stir in diced vegetables, shredded cheese, salt, and pepper.

Microwave on medium-high for 2-3 minutes, until the frittata is set.

NUTRIENT-RICH LUNCH RECIPES

Microwaveable Macaroni and Cheese:

Ingredients

1 cup macaroni pasta

1/2 cup shredded cheddar cheese

1/2 cup milk (dairy or non-dairy)

1/4 tsp salt

1/4 tsp black pepper

Instructions

Cook the macaroni pasta according to package instructions, then drain.

In a microwave-safe bowl, combine the cooked pasta, shredded cheese, milk, salt, and pepper.

Microwave on medium-high for 1-2 minutes, stirring occasionally, until the cheese is melted and the mixture is heated through.

Stuffed Baked Potato with Toppings:

Ingredients

1 large russet potato

1/4 cup shredded cheese

2 tbsp sour cream

2 tbsp chopped green onions

Salt and pepper to taste

Instructions

Wash the potato, pierce it with a fork a few times, and microwave on high for 5-7 minutes, until tender.

Cut open the potato and fluff the inside with a fork.

Top with shredded cheese, sour cream, chopped green onions, salt, and pepper.

Microwaved Vegetable Stir-Fry with Tofu:

Ingredients

1 cup mixed vegetables (e.g., bell peppers, broccoli, carrots)

1/2 cup firm tofu, cubed

2 tbsp stir-fry sauce

1 tbsp vegetable oil

Instructions

In a microwave-safe bowl, toss the mixed vegetables, tofu, stir-fry sauce, and vegetable oil.

Microwave on high for 3-4 minutes, stirring halfway through, until the vegetables are tender and the tofu is heated through.

Instant Cup Noodles or Ramen:

Ingredients

1 instant cup of noodles or ramen

Water

Instructions

Remove the lid and seasoning packet from the cup.

Fill the cup with water according to the fill line.

Microwave on high for 2-3 minutes, until the noodles are cooked.

Stir in the seasoning packet and enjoy.

Microwaved Leftovers from Dinner:

Ingredients

Leftovers from a previous dinner

Instructions

Place the leftovers in a microwave-safe container.

Heat on medium-high for 2-3 minutes, or until heated through.

Stir and enjoy.

Microwaveable Chicken or Veggie Wrap:

Ingredients

1 large tortilla

Cooked chicken or sautéed vegetables

2 tbsp hummus or dressing

Lettuce or spinach

Instructions

Lay the tortilla on a microwave-safe plate.

Spread hummus or dressing onto the tortilla.

Layer with cooked chicken or sautéed vegetables and lettuce or spinach.

Roll up the tortilla, and microwave on medium for 30 seconds to warm it.

Quick Microwave Burrito Bowl:

Ingredients

1/2 cup cooked rice

1/2 cup black beans (canned or cooked)

1/4 cup diced tomatoes

1/4 cup shredded cheese

1 tbsp chopped cilantro

Squeeze of lime juice

Instructions

In a microwave-safe bowl, combine the cooked rice, black beans, diced tomatoes, and shredded cheese.

Microwave on medium-high for 1-2 minutes, until the cheese is melted and the mixture is heated through.

Top with chopped cilantro and a squeeze of lime juice.

Microwaved Spinach and Feta Stuffed Chicken Breast:

Ingredients

1 boneless, skinless chicken breast

1/4 cup cooked spinach

2 tbsp crumbled feta cheese

Salt and pepper to taste

Instructions

Cut a pocket in the chicken breast by slicing it horizontally but not all the way through.

Stuff the chicken breast with cooked spinach and crumbled feta cheese.

Season with salt and pepper.

Microwave on medium-high for 4-5 minutes, or until the chicken is cooked through.

Instant Microwaveable Soup or Chili:

Ingredients

1 cup instant soup or chili (pre-packaged)

Water

Instructions

Empty the contents of the instant soup or chili into a microwave-safe bowl.

Add water according to package instructions.

Microwave on high for the specified time on the package, usually 2-3 minutes.

Stir and let it cool slightly before enjoying.

Microwaveable Vegetable Lasagna:

Ingredients

1 slice of pre-made vegetable lasagna

Shredded mozzarella cheese (optional)

Instructions

Place the slice of vegetable lasagna on a microwave-safe plate.

Microwave on medium-high for 3-4 minutes, or until heated through.

If desired, sprinkle shredded mozzarella cheese on top and microwave for an additional 1-2 minutes until melted.

Microwaved Quinoa and Black Bean Bowl:

Ingredients

1/2 cup cooked quinoa

1/2 cup black beans (canned or cooked)

1/4 cup diced avocado

2 tbsp salsa

Chopped cilantro (optional)

Instructions

In a microwave-safe bowl, combine the cooked quinoa and black beans.

Microwave on medium-high for 1-2 minutes, until heated.

Top with diced avocado, salsa, and chopped cilantro if desired.

Teriyaki Chicken with Steamed Rice:

Ingredients

1 boneless, skinless chicken breast, sliced

2 tbsp teriyaki sauce

1/2 cup cooked white or brown rice

Steamed broccoli (optional)

Instructions

Toss the sliced chicken breast with teriyaki sauce in a microwave-safe bowl.

Microwave on medium-high for 3-4 minutes, or until the chicken is cooked through.

Serve over cooked rice and steamed broccoli if desired.

Microwaved Stuffed Bell Peppers:

Ingredients

2 bell peppers, halved and seeds removed

1 cup cooked ground meat (beef, turkey, etc.)

1/2 cup cooked rice

1/4 cup diced tomatoes

Shredded cheese for topping

Instructions

Place the bell pepper halves in a microwave-safe dish.

Mix the cooked ground meat, cooked rice, and diced tomatoes.

Stuff the bell pepper halves with the mixture.

Microwave on medium-high for 3-4 minutes, until the peppers are tender and the filling is heated.

Top with shredded cheese and microwave for an additional 1-2 minutes until melted.

Microwaveable Pasta with Marinara Sauce and Vegetables:

Ingredients

1 cup cooked pasta

1/2 cup marinara sauce

1/4 cup diced vegetables (e.g., bell peppers, zucchini)

Instructions

In a microwave-safe bowl, combine the cooked pasta, marinara sauce, and diced vegetables.

Microwave on medium-high for 1-2 minutes, stirring occasionally, until heated.

Quick Microwave Quesadilla with Cheese and Beans:

Ingredients

2 small flour tortillas

1/2 cup shredded cheese

1/4 cup black beans (canned or cooked)

Instructions

Place one tortilla on a microwave-safe plate and sprinkle half of the shredded cheese on it.

Top with black beans and the remaining cheese.

Place the second tortilla on top and microwave on medium-high for 1-2 minutes, until the cheese is melted and the quesadilla is heated through.

Microwaved Egg Fried Rice with Veggies:

Ingredients

1 cup cooked white or brown rice

1 large egg, beaten

1/4 cup diced mixed vegetables (e.g., carrots, peas, corn)

Soy sauce to taste

Instructions

In a microwave-safe bowl, mix the cooked rice, beaten egg, and diced vegetables.

Microwave on medium-high for 2-3 minutes, stirring occasionally, until the egg is cooked and the rice is heated.

Drizzle with soy sauce and enjoy.

NUTRIENT-RICH DINNER RECIPES

Microwaved Baked Potato with Toppings:

Ingredients

1 large russet potato

Toppings of your choice (e.g., butter, sour cream, cheese, chives)

Instructions

Wash the potato and pierce it with a fork a few times.

Place the potato on a microwave-safe plate and microwave on high for 5-7 minutes, until tender.

Cut open the potato, fluff the inside with a fork, and add your preferred toppings.

Instant Microwaveable Dinner Entrée:

Ingredients

1 instant microwaveable dinner entrée (e.g., frozen meal)

Instructions

Remove the packaging from the dinner entrée.

Follow the cooking instructions on the package, usually involving microwaving on high for a specified time.

Allow the meal to cool slightly before enjoying.

Microwaved Chicken and Vegetable Stir-Fry:

Ingredients

1 boneless, skinless chicken breast, sliced

1 cup mixed vegetables (e.g., bell peppers, broccoli, carrots)

2 tbsp stir-fry sauce

1 tbsp vegetable oil

Instructions

In a microwave-safe bowl, toss the sliced chicken breast, mixed vegetables, stir-fry sauce, and vegetable oil.

Microwave on medium-high for 3-4 minutes, stirring halfway through, until the chicken is cooked through and the vegetables are tender.

Quick Microwave Pasta with Sauce:

Ingredients

1 cup cooked pasta

1/2 cup pasta sauce

Grated Parmesan cheese (optional)

Instructions

In a microwave-safe bowl, combine the cooked pasta and pasta sauce.

Microwave on medium-high for 1-2 minutes, stirring occasionally, until heated.

Sprinkle with grated Parmesan cheese if desired.

Microwaved Stuffed Bell Peppers:

Ingredients

2 bell peppers, halved and seeds removed

1 cup cooked ground meat (beef, turkey, etc.)

1/2 cup cooked rice

1/4 cup diced tomatoes

Shredded cheese for topping

Instructions

Place the bell pepper halves in a microwave-safe dish.

Mix the cooked ground meat, cooked rice, and diced tomatoes.

Stuff the bell pepper halves with the mixture.

Microwave on medium-high for 3-4 minutes, until the peppers are tender and the filling is heated.

Top with shredded cheese and microwave for an additional 1-2 minutes until melted.

Microwaveable Beef or Vegetable Stew:

Ingredients

1 cup beef or vegetable stew (pre-packaged or homemade)

Instructions

Transfer the stew into a microwave-safe bowl.

Microwave on medium-high for 3-4 minutes, stirring occasionally, until heated through.

Let it cool slightly before enjoying.

Microwaved Salmon with Lemon and Herbs:

Ingredients

1 salmon fillet

Lemon slices

Fresh herbs (e.g., dill, parsley)

Salt and pepper to taste

Instructions

Place the salmon fillet on a microwave-safe plate.

Season with salt and pepper, and top with lemon slices and fresh herbs.

Microwave on medium-high for 3-4 minutes, until the salmon flakes easily with a fork.

Instant Microwaveable Pizza:

Ingredients

1 individual-sized microwaveable pizza

Instructions

Remove the pizza from its packaging.

Place the pizza on a microwave-safe plate.

Follow the microwave cooking instructions on the package to heat the pizza.

Microwaveable Vegetable Curry with Rice:

Ingredients

1 cup cooked rice

1/2 cup microwaveable vegetable curry (pre-packaged or homemade)

Instructions

Transfer the vegetable curry into a microwave-safe bowl.

Microwave on medium-high for 2-3 minutes, stirring occasionally, until heated through.

Serve over cooked rice.

Microwaved Sweet and Sour Chicken:

Ingredients

1 cup cooked chicken chunks

1/4 cup sweet and sour sauce

1/2 cup mixed vegetables (e.g., bell peppers, pineapple)

Instructions

In a microwave-safe bowl, combine the cooked chicken chunks, sweet and sour sauce, and mixed vegetables.

Microwave on medium-high for 2-3 minutes, stirring occasionally, until heated through.

Microwaved Spinach and Cheese Stuffed Pasta:

Ingredients

1 cup cooked spinach and cheese stuffed pasta (e.g., ravioli)

Instructions

Transfer the cooked stuffed pasta into a microwave-safe bowl.

Microwave on medium-high for 2-3 minutes, until heated through.

Toss with additional sauce if desired.

Quick Microwave Ramen Bowl with Veggies and Protein:

Ingredients

1 package instant ramen noodles

Mixed vegetables (e.g., sliced carrots, snow peas)

Cooked protein (e.g., cooked chicken, tofu)

Instructions

Place the instant ramen noodles and mixed vegetables in a microwave-safe bowl.

Add water according to the package instructions.

Microwave on high for 2-3 minutes, until the noodles are cooked.

Add the cooked protein and the seasoning packet, and stir well.

Microwaveable Chicken or Vegetable Pot Pie:

Ingredients

1 individual-sized microwaveable chicken or vegetable pot pie

Instructions

Remove the pot pie from its packaging.

Place the pot pie on a microwave-safe plate.

Follow the microwave cooking instructions on the package to heat the pot pie.

Microwaved Quinoa and Roasted Vegetables:

Ingredients

1 cup cooked quinoa

Roasted vegetables (e.g., zucchini, bell peppers, onions)

Olive oil and seasonings

Instructions

In a microwave-safe bowl, combine the cooked quinoa and roasted vegetables.

Drizzle with olive oil and seasonings to taste.

Microwave on medium-high for 2-3 minutes, stirring occasionally, until heated through.

Microwaveable Black Bean and Corn Enchiladas:

Ingredients

2 microwaveable black bean and corn enchiladas (pre-packaged)

Instructions

Remove the enchiladas from their packaging.

Place the enchiladas on a microwave-safe plate.

Follow the microwave cooking instructions on the package to heat the enchiladas.

NUTRIENT-RICH SNACK RECIPES

Microwaveable Popcorn:

Ingredients

Microwave popcorn bag

Instructions

Place the microwave popcorn bag in the center of the microwave.

Follow the instructions on the popcorn bag for cooking times.

Remove the bag carefully from the microwave, open, and enjoy freshly popped popcorn.

Warm Nachos with Melted Cheese:

Ingredients

Tortilla chips

Shredded cheese

Optional toppings (e.g., jalapenos, salsa, sour cream)

Instructions

Spread a layer of tortilla chips on a microwave-safe plate.

Sprinkle shredded cheese over the chips.

Microwave on medium-high for about 30-60 seconds, until the cheese is melted.

Add your favorite toppings and enjoy warm nachos.

Microwaved Baked Apple with Cinnamon:

Ingredients

1 apple, cored and sliced

Ground cinnamon

Optional toppings (e.g., honey, chopped nuts)

Instructions

Place the apple slices in a microwave-safe bowl.

Sprinkle with ground cinnamon.

Microwave on high for 1-2 minutes, until the apple slices are tender.

Drizzle with honey and sprinkle with chopped nuts if desired.

Mini Microwave Mug Cake:

Ingredients

4 tbsp all-purpose flour

2 tbsp sugar

1/8 tsp baking powder

Pinch of salt

3 tbsp milk (dairy or non-dairy)

1 tbsp oil

1/4 tsp vanilla extract

Optional mix-ins (e.g., chocolate chips, nuts)

Instructions

In a microwave-safe mug, whisk together the flour, sugar, baking powder, and salt.

Add milk, oil, and vanilla extract. Stir until smooth.

If desired, fold in optional mix-ins.

Microwave on high for 1-2 minutes, until the cake is cooked and firm.

Toasted Microwave Quesadilla with Cheese:

Ingredients

2 small flour tortillas

Shredded cheese

Optional fillings (e.g., chopped veggies, cooked chicken)

Instructions

Place one tortilla on a microwave-safe plate.

Sprinkle shredded cheese and optional fillings on one half of the tortilla.

Fold the other half over the cheese and fillings to create a half-moon shape.

Microwave on medium-high for about 1-2 minutes, until the cheese is melted and the quesadilla is toasted.

Microwaved Mixed Nuts with Spices:

Ingredients

Mixed nuts (e.g., almonds, cashews, walnuts)

Olive oil or melted butter

Spices (e.g., paprika, cayenne pepper, garlic powder)

Instructions

In a microwave-safe bowl, toss the mixed nuts with a drizzle of olive oil or melted butter.

Sprinkle with desired spices and stir to coat.

Microwave on medium-high in 30-second intervals, stirring in between, until the nuts are toasted and fragrant.

Quick Microwave Potato Chips:

Ingredients

1 potato, thinly sliced

Olive oil

Salt

Instructions

Place the potato slices in a single layer on a microwave-safe plate.

Lightly brush or drizzle with olive oil and sprinkle with salt.

Microwave on high for 2-3 minutes, until the potato slices are crisp and golden.

Microwaved Mozzarella Sticks:

Ingredients

Mozzarella cheese sticks

Breadcrumbs

Egg wash (1 beaten egg)

Instructions

Dip each mozzarella cheese stick in egg wash and then coat with breadcrumbs.

Place the coated cheese sticks on a microwave-safe plate.

Microwave on medium-high for about 1-2 minutes, until the cheese is melted and the breadcrumbs are golden and crispy.

Warm Nut Butter on Rice Cakes:

Ingredients

Rice cakes

Nut butter (e.g., peanut butter, almond butter)

Instructions

Spread a layer of nut butter on a rice cake.

Microwave on medium for about 15-20 seconds, until the nut butter is warm and slightly melted.

Enjoy your warm and nutty rice cake snack.

Microwaveable Trail Mix with Dried Fruits:

Ingredients

Mixed nuts and seeds

Dried fruits (e.g., raisins, cranberries, apricots)

Instructions

Combine mixed nuts, seeds, and dried fruits in a microwave-safe bowl.

Microwave on medium in 30-second intervals, stirring in between, until the nuts are toasted and the dried fruits are slightly softened.

Microwaved Mini Pizza on English Muffin:

Ingredients

1 English muffin, halved

Pizza sauce

Shredded cheese

Pizza toppings (e.g., pepperoni, olives, bell peppers)

Instructions

Place the English muffin halves on a microwave-safe plate.

Spread pizza sauce on each muffin half.

Sprinkle shredded cheese and add your preferred pizza toppings.

Microwave on medium-high for about 1-2 minutes, until the cheese is melted and bubbly.

Melted Chocolate-Dipped Strawberries:

Ingredients

Fresh strawberries

Chocolate chips or chopped chocolate

Instructions

Melt the chocolate chips or chopped chocolate in the microwave in 20-second intervals, stirring in between, until smooth.

Dip each strawberry into the melted chocolate, coating about half of the strawberry.

Place the chocolate-dipped strawberries on a plate and refrigerate for a few minutes to set.

Microwaved Yogurt and Granola Parfait:

Ingredients

Greek yogurt

Granola

Fresh berries or fruits

Instructions

Layer Greek yogurt, granola, and fresh berries or fruits in a microwave-safe bowl.

Microwave on medium for about 20-30 seconds, just enough to slightly warm the yogurt and berries.

Toasted Microwave Pita Chips with Hummus:

Ingredients

Pita bread, cut into triangles

Olive oil

Salt

Hummus for dipping

Instructions

Arrange the pita triangles in a single layer on a microwave-safe plate.

Lightly brush or drizzle with olive oil and sprinkle with salt.

Microwave on high for about 1-2 minutes, until the pita chips are toasted and crisp.

Serve with hummus for dipping.

Quick Microwave Oat Bars:

Ingredients

1 cup old-fashioned oats

1/4 cup honey or maple syrup

1/4 cup nut butter (e.g., peanut butter, almond butter)

Optional mix-ins (e.g., chocolate chips, dried fruits, nuts)

Instructions

In a microwave-safe bowl, combine oats, honey or maple syrup, and nut butter.

Add any optional mix-ins and stir to combine.

Microwave on medium-high for 1-2 minutes, until the mixture is set.

Let it cool and firm up before cutting into bars.

NUTRIENT-RICH DESSERT REICPES

Warm Chocolate Chip Cookie in a Mug:

Ingredients

1 tbsp butter

1 tbsp granulated sugar

1 tbsp brown sugar

1/4 tsp vanilla extract

Pinch of salt

1 egg yolk

1/4 cup all-purpose flour

2 tbsp chocolate chips

The Complete Guide to Microwave Cooking 2023

Instructions

In a microwave-safe mug, melt the butter in the microwave.

Stir in granulated sugar, brown sugar, vanilla extract, and salt until well combined.

Add the egg yolk and mix until smooth.

Stir in the flour until just combined, then fold in the chocolate chips.

Microwave on high for about 45-60 seconds, until the cookie is set but slightly gooey in the center.

Microwaved Apple Crisp with Oats:

Ingredients

1 apple, peeled, cored, and chopped

2 tbsp rolled oats

1 tbsp flour

1 tbsp brown sugar

1/4 tsp cinnamon

1 tbsp butter

Instructions

In a microwave-safe bowl, combine the chopped apple, rolled oats, flour, brown sugar, and cinnamon.

Cut the butter into small pieces and distribute them over the apple mixture.

Microwave on high for about 2-3 minutes, until the apples are tender and the topping is crispy.

Quick Microwave Brownie in a Mug:

Ingredients

2 tbsp butter

2 tbsp granulated sugar

1 tbsp cocoa powder

1/4 tsp vanilla extract

Pinch of salt

1 egg

1/4 cup all-purpose flour

1 tbsp chocolate chips (optional)

Instructions

In a microwave-safe mug, melt the butter.

Stir in granulated sugar, cocoa powder, vanilla extract, and salt until well combined.

Add the egg and mix until smooth.

Stir in the flour until just combined, then fold in the chocolate chips.

Microwave on high for about 60-90 seconds, until the brownie is set but still slightly moist.

Instant Microwaveable Chocolate Pudding:

Ingredients

1 package instant chocolate pudding mix

Milk (as per package instructions)

Instructions

Prepare the instant chocolate pudding mix according to the package instructions, using milk.

Microwave the prepared pudding in a microwave-safe dish for about 1-2 minutes, until heated through.

Microwaved Banana Split with Toppings:

Ingredients

1 ripe banana, sliced

Vanilla ice cream

Chocolate sauce

Whipped cream

Chopped nuts and cherries (optional)

Instructions

Place the banana slices in a microwave-safe dish.

Microwave on medium for about 30 seconds, until slightly warmed.

Top the banana slices with vanilla ice cream, chocolate sauce, whipped cream, chopped nuts, and a cherry.

Warm Fruit Cobbler with Ice Cream:

Ingredients

1 cup mixed berries or fruit

2 tbsp granulated sugar

1/4 cup all-purpose flour

1/4 cup rolled oats

2 tbsp butter

Vanilla ice cream

Instructions

In a microwave-safe bowl, toss the mixed berries or fruit with granulated sugar.

In a separate bowl, mix the flour, rolled oats, and butter until crumbly.

Sprinkle the crumble mixture over the fruit.

Microwave on high for about 2-3 minutes, until the fruit is bubbly and the topping is golden.

Serve warm with a scoop of vanilla ice cream.

Microwaved Rice Pudding with Cinnamon:

Ingredients

1/4 cup cooked rice

1 cup milk (dairy or non-dairy)

2 tbsp sugar

1/4 tsp ground cinnamon

Instructions

In a microwave-safe bowl, combine the cooked rice, milk, sugar, and ground cinnamon.

Microwave on medium-high for 3-4 minutes, stirring occasionally, until the mixture thickens.

Microwaveable S'mores Dip:

Ingredients

Chocolate chips

Mini marshmallows

Graham crackers

Instructions

In a microwave-safe dish, layer chocolate chips and mini marshmallows.

Microwave on medium-high in 30-second intervals, until the chocolate is melted and the marshmallows are puffed and golden.

Serve with graham crackers for dipping.

Easy Microwave Caramel Popcorn:

Ingredients

1 bag of microwave popcorn (popped)

1/4 cup caramel sauce

Instructions

Pop the microwave popcorn according to package instructions.

Drizzle the caramel sauce over the popped popcorn.

Microwave on medium in 20-second intervals, stirring in between, until the caramel is warm and coats the popcorn.

Microwaved Bread Pudding with Raisins:

Ingredients

2 slices of bread, cubed

1/4 cup milk (dairy or non-dairy)

1 egg

2 tbsp granulated sugar

1/4 tsp vanilla extract

2 tbsp raisins

Instructions

In a microwave-safe bowl, combine the bread cubes, milk, egg, granulated sugar, vanilla extract, and raisins.

Microwave on medium-high for about 2-3 minutes, until the pudding is set and no longer runny.

Quick Microwave Berry Crumble:

Ingredients

1 cup mixed berries (fresh or frozen)

2 tbsp granulated sugar

2 tbsp all-purpose flour

2 tbsp rolled oats

1 tbsp butter

Instructions

In a microwave-safe bowl, toss the mixed berries with granulated sugar.

In a separate bowl, mix the flour, rolled oats, and butter until crumbly.

Sprinkle the crumble mixture over the berries.

Microwave on high for about 2-3 minutes, until the berries are bubbly and the topping is golden.

Microwaved Chocolate-Covered Strawberries:

Ingredients

Fresh strawberries

Chocolate chips or chopped chocolate

Instructions

Melt the chocolate chips or chopped chocolate in the microwave in 20-second intervals, stirring in between, until smooth.

Dip each strawberry into the melted chocolate, coating about two-thirds of the strawberry.

Place the chocolate-covered strawberries on a plate and refrigerate for a few minutes to set.

Warm Cinnamon Roll in a Mug:

Ingredients

1 refrigerated cinnamon roll dough

Icing from cinnamon roll package

Instructions

Place the cinnamon roll dough in a microwave-safe mug.

Microwave on high for about 1 minute, until the cinnamon roll is cooked and puffed.

Drizzle the icing over the warm cinnamon roll.

Microwaveable Cheesecake in a Cup:

Ingredients

1/4 cup cream cheese

2 tbsp granulated sugar

1/4 tsp vanilla extract

1 egg

Graham cracker crumbs (optional)

Instructions

In a microwave-safe cup, mix cream cheese, granulated sugar, and vanilla extract until smooth.

Add the egg and mix until well combined.

Microwave on medium-high for about 1-2 minutes, until the cheesecake is set.

Optionally, sprinkle graham cracker crumbs on top before serving.

Microwaved Fruit Fondue with Chocolate:

Ingredients

Assorted fresh fruits (e.g., strawberries, bananas, apple slices)

Chocolate chips or chopped chocolate

Instructions

Melt the chocolate chips or chopped chocolate in the microwave in 20-second intervals, stirring in between, until smooth.

Arrange the fresh fruits on a plate.

Dip the fruits into the melted chocolate for a delicious fondue experience.

CHAPTER V: FINAL NOTES BEFORE YOU GO!

Bringing our microwave cooking exploration to a close, I want to express my deepest gratitude to you for coming along for the ride. More than just a collection of recipes, the information presented here has opened up a world of time-saving, imaginative, and scrumptious culinary possibilities.

Since its inception as a simple method for reheating, microwave cooking has come a long way. It has proven that flavor and health do not have to be sacrificed for the sake of convenience. You've mastered the microwave's transformative potential by exploring these ideas for fast, healthy dinners.

With this cookbook closed and your return to the kitchen imminent, may the insights and ideas contained herein bring you renewed enthusiasm and ease in the kitchen. Your particular dietary tastes and nutritional demands may be met by using the concepts of preparation, experimentation, and customization to your cooking.

Keep in mind that the microwave is great because it allows you to create a symphony of tastes, smells, and textures in a fraction of the time. It's about overcoming prejudices in the kitchen, expanding your horizons creatively, and savoring the thrill of discovery with every taste.

This cookbook has been with you every step of the way as you've learned to master the art of microwave cooking. Take these lessons with you as you explore the world of food on your own. Think of each meal as an opportunity to experiment and use the microwave as a blank canvas for your culinary masterpieces.

Your faith in this cookbook is much appreciated. We hope you continue to find joy in the kitchen and that the scent of your delicious meals inspires you to experiment with new recipes. Cheers to the future of microwave cooking, where there will be no more complicated preparations and no end to the variety of tastes you may enjoy in your home.

Exploring Nutrient-Rich Ingredients

Discovering new, nutrient-dense foods for microwave cooking opens up a world of options beyond the traditional idea of fast and easy meals. These ingredients not only add zest to your cooking, but they also provide a healthy dose of vitamins, minerals, and antioxidants. Including these nutrient-dense ingredients in your microwave-friendly meals is a proactive step toward supporting your health while appreciating the convenience of microwave cooking.

Rich in vitamins A, C, and K and minerals like iron and calcium, leafy greens such as spinach, kale, and Swiss chard are nutritious powerhouses. They may be cooked quickly in the microwave and served as a side dish, or added to other dishes like omelets, soups, and stir-fries to increase the nutritious value.

Vegetables with bright colors, such as bell peppers, carrots, and sweet potatoes, have high concentrations of antioxidants and other beneficial compounds. These veggies are great for salads, roasts, and other recipes since their color and nutrition are preserved in the microwave.

Blueberries, strawberries, and raspberries are just a few examples of the berry fruits that are loaded with the health-promoting antioxidants known as polyphenols. Add them to your morning bowl of oatmeal or yogurt, or use them to whip up some fast sweets in the microwave that will satisfy your sweet tooth and your body's need for nutrition.

Skinless chicken, fish, and tofu are all good examples of lean proteins to choose. The saturated fat content of these protein sources is low, while their necessary amino acid content is substantial. Whether you're cooking a salad, a wrap, or a major dish, microwaving lean meats keeps them soft and moist.

Almonds, chia seeds, and flaxseeds are just a few examples of nuts and seeds that may be used to give your meals a crunchier texture and a nutritional boost. Use them as a topping for yogurt or cereal, or include them into energy bars that can be heated in the microwave.

Grains that have not been refined include oats, quinoa, and brown rice, all of which are whole grains. Use them as the foundation for everything from grain bowls to pilafs, all of which can be prepared in a microwave.

Beans, lentils, and chickpeas are just a few examples of legumes that are high-quality plant-based protein, fiber, and nutritional sources. Put them in the microwave to make substantial and healthy soups, stews, and salads.

Add some herbs and spices to your microwave meals to boost the flavor and health benefits. Herbs and spices are used to give food more flavor, but many of them also have health advantages of their own.

Greek yogurt is a protein and probiotic powerhouse, and it can be used in a wide variety of recipes. Spread it on toast for breakfast or sprinkle it on top of your dessert.

The avocado is a fruit that is rich in many different nutrients, including healthy fats, fiber, and a number of different vitamins and minerals. Spread it over toast or use it as a creamy topping for a variety of foods after mashing it.

You can take your microwave cooking to the next level of healthfulness by experimenting with these nutrient-dense ingredients. You may take advantage of the microwave's speed and convenience while still getting the nutrition you need by preparing healthy meals like these.

Printed in Great Britain
by Amazon